The Nature Boy
Pro Wrestler
Ric Flair

by Angie Peterson Kaelberer

Reading Consultant:
Dr. Robert Miller
Professor of Special Education
Minnesota State University, Mankato

CAPSTONE
HIGH-INTEREST
BOOKS

an imprint of Capstone Press
Mankato, Minnesota

Capstone High-Interest Books are published by Capstone Press
151 Good Counsel Drive, P.O. Box 669, Mankato, Minnesota 56002
http://www.capstone-press.com

Library of Congress Cataloging-in-Publication Data
Kaelberer, Angie Peterson.
The nature boy: pro wrestler Ric Flair / by Angie Peterson Kaelberer.
    p. cm.—(Pro wrestlers)
    Summary: Traces the life and career of the professional wrestler Ric Flair.
Includes bibliographical references and index.
    ISBN 0-7368-2141-4 (hardcover)
    1. Flair, Ric, 1949– —Juvenile literature. 2. Wrestlers—United States—
Biography—Juvenile literature. [1. Flair, Ric, 1949– 2. Wrestlers.] I. Title.
II. Series.
GV1196.F59K34 2004
796.812'092—dc21   2003001051

Editorial Credits

Karen Risch, product planning editor; Timothy Halldin, series designer;
    Patrick Dentinger, book designer; Jo Miller, photo researcher

Photo Credits

Dr. Michael Lano, cover inset (left), 7, 13, 15, 16, 23, 24, 26, 28, 31, 33, 34, 42
Getty Images/NBAE, cover (main)
Michael Blair, cover inset (right), 4, 10, 19, 20, 36, 39, 41

1 2 3 4 5 6 08 07 06 05 04 03

Capstone Press thanks Dr. Michael Lano, WReaLano@aol.com, for his assistance in the
preparation of this book.

Table of Contents

Chapter 1

NWA Champion

On May 7, 1989, pro wrestling fans gathered at the Municipal Auditorium in Nashville, Tennessee. The fans were there to watch a National Wrestling Alliance (NWA) event called WrestleWar.

Richard Fliehr walked into the ring. He wrestles under the name Ric Flair. Ric was there to wrestle NWA World Champion Richard Blood, who wrestled as Ricky Steamboat.

The match was an important one for both wrestlers. Earlier in the year, they had wrestled twice for the title. Both times, Steamboat defeated Ric. In Nashville, Ric was determined to win back the title.

In 1989, Ric wanted to win back the NWA World Championship at WrestleWar.

A Judged Match

Pro wrestling matches do not usually have judges. But at WrestleWar, wrestlers Terry Funk, Lou Thesz, and Pat O'Connor sat beside the ring to act as judges. The judges would decide the winner if neither wrestler scored a pin within one hour.

Steamboat controlled most of the early action in the match. Later in the match, Ric pushed Steamboat out of the ring and took him down with a suplex. Ric wrapped his arms around Steamboat and fell back. Ric then pulled Steamboat up onto the apron. Steamboat dropped to the floor behind him. Steamboat then nearly took Ric down with a reverse roll.

Back in the ring, Steamboat climbed to the top rope and took Ric down with a flying chop. Steamboat got up on the top rope again. Ric fell against the ropes and knocked Steamboat to the floor.

Ric followed Steamboat out of the ring. Ric used a suplex off the apron to throw Steamboat back into the ring. Ric then used his signature move, the figure-four leglock. As Steamboat lay on his back, Ric pushed his left foot

At WrestleWar, Ric's opponent was Ricky "the Dragon" Steamboat.

between Steamboat's legs. Ric bent Steamboat's right leg at the knee. He positioned Steamboat's right leg over the left leg. Steamboat's legs looked like they formed the number four. Ric then lay down on his back and stretched his right leg over Steamboat's lower right leg.

Ric held Steamboat down with the figure-four leglock for nearly one minute. Steamboat then got out of Ric's hold. Ric grabbed Steamboat's leg, and Steamboat kicked him to the mat. Steamboat pulled Ric up and prepared to slam him on the mat. Instead, Steamboat fell forward onto the mat. Ric covered him for the pin as the referee counted to three. The judges did not have to decide the match. Ric was the new NWA World Champion.

About Ric Flair

Ric Flair is 6 feet, 1 inch (185 centimeters) tall and weighs 243 pounds (110 kilograms). He began his wrestling career in 1972. Besides the NWA, he has wrestled for the American Wrestling Association (AWA), World Championship Wrestling (WCW), and World Wrestling Entertainment (WWE). Before May 2002, WWE was called the World Wrestling Federation (WWF).

Ric has won many titles during his career. They include two WWF World Championships, eight NWA World Championships, and eight WCW World Championships. His eight World Championships are a WCW record.

Major Matches

September 17, 1981—Ric defeats Dusty Rhodes to win the NWA World Championship.

November 24, 1983—Ric defeats Harley Race to win his second NWA World Championship.

May 7, 1989—Ric defeats Ricky Steamboat to win his seventh NWA World Championship.

January 11, 1991—Ric defeats Sting to become the first WCW World Champion.

January 19, 1992—Ric wins the Royal Rumble to become the WWF World Champion.

September 1, 1992—Ric defeats Randy Savage to win his second WWF World Championship.

March 14, 1999—Ric defeats Hulk Hogan to win his sixth WCW World Championship.

May 29, 2000—Ric sets a WCW record by becoming the first eight-time WCW World Champion.

January 20, 2002—Ric defeats Vince McMahon in a street fight at the Royal Rumble.

Chapter 2

The Early Years

Ric was born February 25, 1949, in Minneapolis, Minnesota. His father, Dick, was a doctor. His mother, Kay, was a writer who worked for a marketing company. Ric was their only child.

Ric grew up in Edina, Minnesota. He liked sports better than school. Dick and Kay worried about Ric's poor grades. In high school, they sent him to Wayland Academy. This private boarding school is in Beaver Dam, Wisconsin.

At Wayland, Ric's grades improved. He also found time for sports. Ric played basketball and football. He also was a champion wrestler.

Ric was born in 1949 in Minneapolis, Minnesota.

College Years

In 1968, Ric graduated from Wayland. He wanted to return to Minnesota for college.

Ric won a scholarship to play football at the University of Minnesota in Minneapolis. He played offensive guard and defensive tackle. Ric spent more time playing football and going to parties than he did studying. He lost his scholarship because of poor grades. Ric quit college in the middle of his second year. He did not know what he was going to do next.

A New Career

At college, Ric had become friends with Greg Gagne. Greg's father is former pro wrestler Verne Gagne, who owned the American Wrestling Association (AWA) in Minneapolis. This wrestling company put on wrestling shows in the Minneapolis area. These matches were shown on TV in Minnesota and other parts of the country. Verne Gagne also ran a wrestling school in Minneapolis. In 1972, Ric joined Gagne's school.

Ric began training as a pro wrestler in 1972.

Ric trained hard at Gagne's school. After a few months, Gagne decided Ric was ready for his first match. On December 10, 1972, Ric wrestled George "Scrap Iron" Gadaski in Rice Lake, Wisconsin. The match ended in a draw.

On January 6, 1973, Ric won his first match. He defeated John Hedimann in St. Paul, Minnesota.

Ric wrestled for the AWA for nearly two years, but he never got the chance to wrestle for a championship. In 1974, North Carolina wrestling promoter Jim Crockett offered Ric a job. Crockett's company was part of the NWA. Ric wanted to become a star. He decided to take Crockett's offer.

The NWA

After he joined the NWA, Ric changed his look. He grew his hair long and bleached it blond. He wore long robes covered with sequins and feathers into the ring. He started to call himself "The Nature Boy." He challenged other wrestlers by saying, "To be the man, you have to beat the man."

Ric Flair's Hero:
Buddy Rogers

Besides Ric, another wrestler was called "The Nature Boy." That wrestler was Buddy Rogers. Rogers' real name was Herman Rohde. He was born in 1921 and began wrestling in 1939.

Rogers won several titles during his long career. In 1961, he won the NWA World Championship. He held this title for nearly two years. In 1963, he became the first World Wide Wrestling Federation (WWWF) World Champion. This company is now WWE.

Rogers retired from active wrestling in 1963. In the 1970s, he managed wrestlers Jimmy "Superfly" Snuka and Ken Patera.

In 1979, Ric wrestled his hero. Ric defeated Rogers in Greensboro, North Carolina.

Later in his career, Rogers continued to manage wrestlers. He died June 26, 1992.

Ric won several championships in the NWA.

Wrestlers play roles during their matches. Some wrestlers are heroes. These wrestlers are called "babyfaces." Other wrestlers act mean to the fans or their opponents. These wrestlers are known as "heels." Ric has played the part of a heel during most of his career.

Ric did well in the NWA. On July 4, 1974, he won his first championship. He teamed with

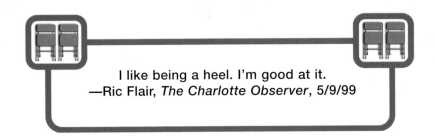

Rip Hawk to defeat Paul Jones and Bob Bruggers for the NWA Mid-Atlantic Tag Team Championship. In 1975, he won two singles titles. On June 3, he defeated Paul Jones for the NWA Television title. On September 20, he defeated Ed "Wahoo" McDaniel to become the NWA Mid-Atlantic Heavyweight Champion.

A Close Call

On October 4, 1975, Ric's wrestling career nearly ended. That night, Ric was flying in a small private airplane to a show in Wilmington, North Carolina. A few miles from Wilmington, the plane ran out of fuel and crashed. The pilot was killed, and the five passengers were injured.

Ric's back was broken in three places. Doctors told Ric that his recovery would take at least one year. They said he probably would never wrestle again.

Ric was determined that his injury would not end his career. He spent many hours each day in physical therapy. He worked hard to regain his strength and speed. On February 1, 1976, wrestling fans were amazed to see Ric in the ring again. He won a match against Wahoo McDaniel.

Ric continued to wrestle well during the late 1970s. In 1977, he teamed with Greg Valentine to win the NWA World Tag Team Championship. That year, he also became the NWA Television Champion and U.S. Champion. In 1978, he again won both of these titles.

Ric had one goal he still had not achieved. He wanted to be the NWA World Champion. Ric began training even harder. He wanted to be ready when the opportunity came to wrestle for the World Championship.

Ric became a star in the NWA.

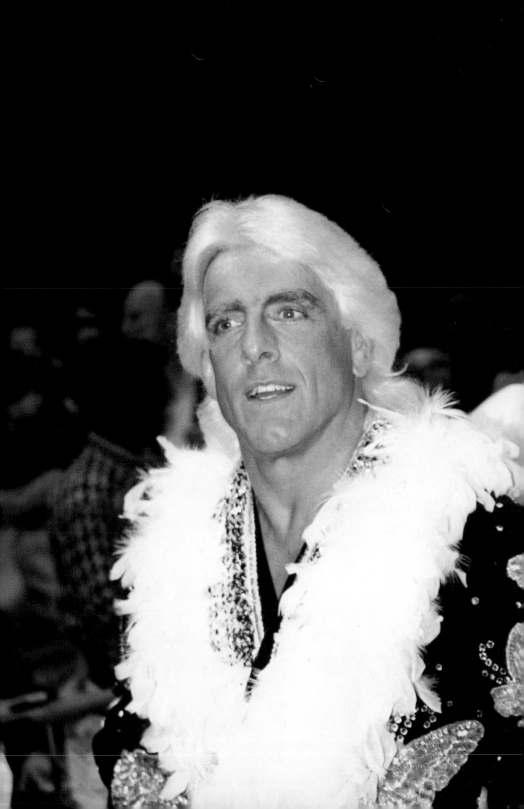

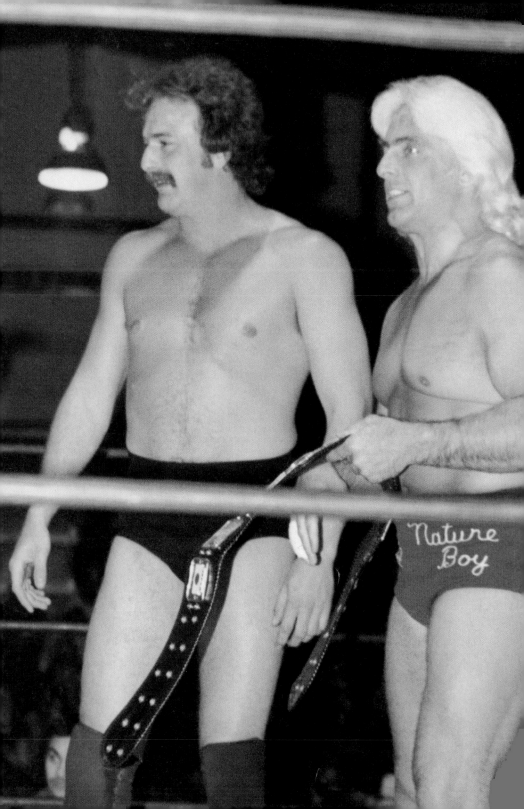

Chapter 3

Wrestling Star

On September 17, 1981, Ric faced NWA World Champion Virgil Runnels Jr. Runnels wrestled as Dusty Rhodes. Ric defeated Rhodes to win his first NWA World Championship.

Ric held the NWA World title for nearly two years. On June 10, 1983, he lost the championship to Harley Race. On November 24, 1983, he challenged Race to a title match. Ric defeated Race to win his second NWA World Championship.

During 1984, Ric won and lost the NWA title two more times. On March 21, Race defeated Ric for the title. Just two days later,

During the early 1980s, Ric competed against Jake "the Snake" Roberts and other top wrestlers.

Ric won the title back from Race. On May 6, Ric lost the title to Kerry Adkisson. Adkisson wrestled as Kerry Von Erich. Later that month, Ric wrestled Von Erich again. This time, Ric won the title. Ric held the World Championship belt for more than two years.

The Four Horsemen

Wrestlers sometimes join together in groups called stables. Wrestlers in stables often wrestle together. They also protect each other during matches.

In 1986, Ric became part of one of the most famous stables in wrestling history. This group was the Four Horsemen. The other members of the Horsemen were Tully Blanchard, Al Rogowski, and Marty Lunde. Rogowski wrestled as Ole Anderson. Lunde was known as Arn Anderson. During the summer of 1986, the other Horsemen helped Ric as he defended his title during several matches.

On July 25, 1986, Dusty Rhodes challenged Ric to a cage match for the title. Since the two wrestlers were locked in a cage, the other Horsemen could not help Ric. He lost the

Ole Anderson (left), Ric, and Arn Anderson (right) were members of the Four Horsemen.

match and the title to Rhodes. Less than two weeks later, Ric wrestled Rhodes for the title again. Ric defeated Rhodes with the figure-four leglock to win his fifth NWA World Championship.

More Championships
Ric held the World Championship belt for more than a year. On September 25, 1987, he

Ric often wrestled Sting during the early 1990s.

lost the title to Ronnie Garvin. In November, he defeated Garvin and regained the title.

Ric held the World Championship throughout 1988. On February 20, 1989, he lost the title to Ricky Steamboat. On May 7, Ric defeated Steamboat to win the World Championship for the seventh time. After the match, Terry Funk attacked Ric. Funk picked up Ric and threw him through a table. Funk's attack hurt Ric's back. He could not wrestle for more than two months.

Once Ric was able to wrestle, he wanted a match with Funk. On November 15, 1989, he defeated Funk at the Clash of the Champions in Troy, New York.

During 1990, Ric's main rival was Steve Borden. Borden wrestles as Sting. On July 7, Sting defeated Ric for the NWA World title.

A New Start

In 1991, TV network owner Ted Turner bought the NWA. He changed its name to World Championship Wrestling. On January 11, 1991, Ric defeated Sting to become the first WCW World Champion. But his new championship did not make him happy. Ric thought that WCW should pay him more than he was earning. WCW officials did not want to pay Ric more money.

In July 1991, Ric left WCW for the WWF. Ric wrestled his first WWF match on September 10, 1991. He defeated Jim Powers in Cornwall, Ontario, Canada.

In the WWF, Ric had some of his best matches with "Macho Man" Randy Savage.

A New Championship

Ric had his first chance to win a WWF title on January 19, 1992. The WWF World Championship had been vacant since November. WWF officials decided that the winner of the 30-man Royal Rumble in January would be the WWF World Champion.

At the Royal Rumble, a new wrestler enters the ring every two minutes. Any wrestler who

> I know that I've had a great career. Whether I'm one of the greatest of all time or not, I'd rather have you say it about myself than me say it.
> —Ric Flair, WWF.com, 11/20/01

is thrown out of the ring is eliminated, until just one wrestler is left.

At the 1992 Rumble, Ric was the third wrestler to enter the ring. He wrestled for more than one hour as he outlasted all 29 other wrestlers. Ric was the WWF World Champion.

Leaving the WWF

Ric held the World Championship belt until April 5, 1992. That night, he lost the title to Randy Poffo at WrestleMania 3. Poffo wrestles as "Macho Man" Randy Savage.

In September, Ric defeated Savage to win his second WWF World Championship. Ric held the title for only one month. In October, Bret Hart defeated Ric for the championship.

Ric was not happy with the WWF. Company officials wanted him to wrestle both tag team and singles matches. Ric wanted to compete only in singles matches.

On February 10, 1993, Ric lost a match to Bret Hart in Germany. Ric then left the WWF and returned to WCW.

Chapter 4

WCW Champion

When Ric returned to WCW, he again became one of the company's top wrestlers. In December 1993, he challenged WCW Champion Leon White to a match. White wrestled as Vader. Ric defeated Vader to win his second WCW World Championship.

Wrestling Hulk Hogan

During the next six months, Ricky Steamboat, Sting, and other wrestlers challenged Ric to title matches. Ric defeated all of them. In June, a wrestler with a career nearly as long as Ric's joined WCW. That wrestler was Terry Bollea, who wrestles as Hulk Hogan.

Ric returned to WCW in 1993.

On July 17, 1994, Ric and Hogan had their first title match. Hogan defeated Ric and took his World Championship.

Ric's loss set up a series of matches between the two wrestlers. On August 24, Ric defeated Hogan to win back the title. WCW officials then decided to have a cage match between Ric and Hogan at Halloween Havoc on October 23. The officials said the losing wrestler would have to retire from wrestling.

Hogan won the match, but Ric did not leave WCW. Instead of wrestling, he managed Vader. Whenever Vader wrestled Hogan, Ric would interfere in the match to try to help Vader win. Hogan finally asked WCW officials to allow Ric to return to wrestling.

A Champion Once More

In December 1995, Ric wrestled WCW World Champion Randy Savage at Starrcade. Ric defeated Savage for the title in less than nine minutes.

On January 22, 1996, Savage won back the belt from Ric. A few weeks later, Ric again defeated Savage for the title.

Ric used the figure-four leglock to defeat Hulk Hogan.

On April 22, Ric lost the World Championship to Paul Wight. At the time, Wight was called the Giant. Today, he wrestles as the Big Show.

In July 1996, Ric won yet another WCW title. He defeated U.S. Champion Charles Ashenoff at Bash at the Beach in Florida. Ashenoff wrestles as Konnan. Ric held the U.S. title for nearly four months.

Hard Times

Late in 1996, Ric hurt his shoulder and needed an operation. Ric could not wrestle while his shoulder healed. He had to give up the U.S. Championship belt.

Ric spent the first months of 1997 training to get back in shape after his operation. He returned to the ring in May 1997.

In early 1998, Ric asked WCW officials for permission to take a night off from wrestling. He wanted to attend his 10-year-old son's wrestling tournament. According to Ric, the officials said he could attend his son's match. But in April, WCW filed a lawsuit against Ric. The officials said they had not given Ric permission to miss the match. WCW president Eric Bischoff then suspended Ric.

Ric's fans were angry with Bischoff's decision. Many fans sent letters and e-mails to WCW asking for Ric's return.

Return to the Ring

In fall 1998, Ric and WCW came to an agreement about the lawsuit. Ric signed a new

Rival in the Ring: Jeff Jarrett

In WCW, Ric often wrestled Jeff Jarrett.

Jarrett was born in 1967 and grew up in Memphis, Tennessee. His father, Jerry Jarrett, is a wrestling promoter. Jeff Jarrett started wrestling in 1986 in Memphis.

In 1993, Jarrett joined the WWF. He won two Intercontinental Championships before leaving to join WCW in late 1996. Jarrett won the WCW U.S. Championship before returning to the WWF in late 1997. During the next two years, Jarrett won three more Intercontinental Championships. He also teamed with Owen Hart to win the WWF Tag Team title.

In August 1999, Jarrett again joined WCW. After WCW was sold, Jarrett and his father formed a new wrestling company in Nashville, Tennessee. The company's name is National Wrestling Alliance/Total Nonstop Action. Jarrett still wrestles for NWA/TNA.

Ric's oldest son, David, also joined WCW.

contract with WCW that paid him about
$2 million over three years.

On September 14, fans stood and cheered as
Ric walked into a WCW ring for the first time
in five months. With tears in his eyes, Ric told
the fans how glad he was to be back.

In early 1999, Ric's 19-year-old son, David, began to wrestle for WCW. Later that year, David won the WCW U.S. Championship. Ric was proud that his son chose to follow him into wrestling.

The End of WCW

In March 1999, Ric won another title. He defeated Hulk Hogan to win his sixth WCW World Championship. He held the title for less than a month before losing it to Page Falkenberg. Falkenberg wrestles as Diamond Dallas Page. Ric won and lost the World Championship belt twice more in 2000.

By early 2001, WCW was in trouble. Fewer people were watching the company's TV shows. The company was losing a great deal of money. WCW's owners decided to sell the company to WWF owner Vince McMahon.

On March 26, 2001, WCW showed its last *Nitro* TV program. Some WCW wrestlers found jobs with the WWF. Ric decided to take some time off from wrestling. He returned to his home in Charlotte, North Carolina.

Chapter 5

Ric Flair Today

On November 19, 2001, the WWF came to Charlotte, North Carolina. At the end of the night, Vince McMahon and wrestler Kurt Angle stood in the ring. As McMahon spoke to the fans, the theme from the movie *2001: A Space Odyssey* began playing. Ric uses this theme as his entrance music.

As the fans cheered, Ric walked down the ramp into the ring. Steve Williams followed him. Williams wrestles as "Stone Cold" Steve Austin. Ric and Austin tossed McMahon and Angle from the ring. Once again, Ric was part of the WWF.

Ric returned to the WWF in 2001.

A New Beginning

Ric had been out of wrestling for about eight months. At 52, he was at least 20 years older than most wrestlers. He needed to get into shape to compete against the younger wrestlers. Ric spent the next two months training. By January, he decided he was ready for his first match.

On January 20, 2002, the Royal Rumble took place in Atlanta, Georgia. Ric faced Vince McMahon in a street fight match. Both men could use pipes, garbage cans, and street signs as weapons in the ring.

McMahon controlled most of the early action in the match. He took down Ric with a figure-four leglock, but Ric got up. McMahon then tried to hit Ric with a metal pipe. Ric defended himself with an uppercut. Later in the match, Ric hit McMahon over the head with the pipe. Ric then put McMahon into the figure-four leglock. In pain, McMahon tapped his hand against the mat. Ric had won the match.

After returning to the WWF, Ric wrestled Chris Jericho.

During the next year, Ric had matches against Paul Levesque, Mark Callaway, Chris Irvine, and other top WWF wrestlers. Levesque wrestles as Triple H. Callaway is the Undertaker. Irvine wrestles as Chris Jericho. Ric did not win any championships. Still, he was happy to be wrestling again.

I feel young. I feel like I'm still contributing to the business. And I still have a passion for it.
—Ric Flair, WWF.com, 11/20/01

Outside the Ring

Ric has lived in Charlotte, North Carolina, for nearly 30 years. He enjoys spending time with his family. Ric and his wife, Beth, have two children, Ashley and Reid. Ric also has two adult children, David and Meaghan, from his first marriage.

Ric has had one of the longest careers in pro wrestling. He could afford to quit wrestling if he wanted. Ric has said that he might run for governor of North Carolina in the future. Even if Ric leaves wrestling for politics, fans will always remember how much he has done for the sport.

In 2002, Ric faced Triple H in the ring. In 2003, he became Triple H's manager.

Career Highlights

1949—Ric is born in Minneapolis, Minnesota.

1972—Ric wrestles his first match for the AWA.

1974—Ric joins the NWA.

1976—Ric returns to the ring just four months after being seriously injured in a plane crash.

1981—Ric wins his first NWA World Championship.

1986—Ric forms the Four Horsemen with Arn Anderson, Ole Anderson, and Tully Blanchard.

1991—Ric becomes the first WCW World Champion; later that year, he joins the WWF.

1992—Ric wins the Royal Rumble to become the WWF World Champion.

1993—Ric returns to WCW and becomes the World Champion.

2000—Ric wins his eighth WCW World title.

2001—Ric returns to the WWF.

Words to Know

injury (IN-juh-ree)—damage or harm to the body

opponent (uh-POH-nuhnt)—a person who competes against another person

physical therapy (FIZ-uh-kuhl THER-uh-pee)—the treatment of diseased or injured muscles and joints with exercise, massage, and heat

sequin (SEE-kwuhn)—a small, shiny object sewn on clothing

signature move (SIG-nuh-chur MOOV)—the move for which a wrestler is best known; this move also is called a finishing move.

stable (STAY-buhl)—a group of wrestlers who protect each other during matches and sometimes wrestle together

To Learn More

Davies, Ross. *Ric Flair.* Wrestling Greats. New York: Rosen, 2001.

Hunter, Matt. *Ric Flair: The Story of the Wrestler They Call "The Nature Boy."* Pro Wrestling Legends. Philadelphia: Chelsea House, 2001.

Kaelberer, Angie Peterson. *Hulk Hogan: Pro Wrestler Terry Bollea.* Pro Wrestlers. Mankato, Minn.: Capstone Press, 2004.

Pope, Kristian, and Ray Whebbe Jr. *The Encyclopedia of Professional Wrestling: 100 Years of the Good, the Bad, and the Unforgettable.* Iola, Wis.: Krause Publications, 2001.

Useful Addresses

Professional Wrestling Hall of Fame
P.O. Box 434
Latham, NY 12110

World Wrestling Entertainment Inc.
1241 East Main Street
Stamford, CT 06902

Internet Sites

Do you want to learn more about Ric Flair?
Visit the FactHound at *http://www.facthound.com*

FactHound can track down many sites to help you. All
the FactHound sites are hand-selected by our editors.
FactHound will fetch the best, most accurate information
to answer your questions.

IT'S EASY! IT'S FUN!
1) Go to *http://www.facthound.com*
2) Type in: 0736821414
3) Click on "FETCH IT" and FactHound will put you on
   the trail of several helpful links.

You can also search by subject or book title. So, relax
and let our pal FactHound do the research for you!

Index